Pottery in Britain today

Michael Casson

POTTERY

IN BRITAIN TODAY

1967/ALEC TIRANTI/LONDON

(C) 1967 ALEC TIRANTI LTD., 72 CHARLOTTE STREET, LONDON, W.1.   PRINTED BY THE DEVONSHIRE PRESS, TORQUAY
MADE AND PRINTED IN THE UNITED KINGDOM   BOUND BY HENRY STEVENSON & CO., LTD., LONDON E.2
GN SBN 85458-020

PREFACE

THE INTENTION of the Author is to give a broad view of the pottery being made by hand in Britain today. The potters represented are not necessarily therefore his personal choice, but are rather a cross section of the many artist craftsmen working here and now. Pottery and not pottery sculpture is the main theme but, as all potters know, the dividing line is not always distinct. The work in clay made by Bryan Newman has been included as an example that is right on one border line—that of pottery and sculpture—while the near-peasant pottery of the Boscean group and the near-industrial beakers by Ken Clark have been included, because they help to define other limits of this selection. What is hoped for is that, by including some lesser known and some younger potters alongside the acknowledged masters, a general but nonetheless accurate picture has been built up of what pottery is like at this time. What lies ahead may perhaps also be divined from some of these reproductions.

Some explanation of the form the book has taken may be necessary. Handbuilding, individual wheel-made pottery, and workshop production (or repetition domestic ware) are the three main divisions. Apart from the fact that most potters' work can be separated into these three main types anyway, the book has been divided in this way because it enables most teacher-potters to contribute to the first two categories. The very nature of their educational work precludes them from showing in the last. It is felt that the potter who is mainly a teacher, who does not have the economic pressures of a workshop to face but who works at a slower pace in some more specialised way, has always been an influence on the pottery movement, and will probably be so to a far more marked degree in the future. They should have adequate consideration in a book of this scope. On the other hand by isolating the production work in the last section it can be seen how few potters work in this—the most exacting medium; they are the life-blood of the movement for it will be their work that is in everyday use in the home.

PHOTOGRAPH CREDITS

INTRODUCTION

THE REVIVAL of non-industrial, that is hand-made, pottery in this country after its near extinction in the face of industrial methods of production and the factory system, is due to many causes. To attribute this rebirth to one cause only is greatly to over-simplify.

Some authorities see the origins of the studio pottery movement in Britain during the latter part of the last century, in the re-awakening of interest in pottery in France. And it is true that at least one direct link between the two countries in this matter can be seen in the teaching of Jean-Charles Cazin who was in London in the 1860s to 1870s. It is on record that he instructed at the Lambeth School of Art where he taught the young Walter Martin—one of the four Martin brothers, early studio potters of individual style. But from the outset the French potters were stimulated by debased examples. Sung pottery was then almost unknown in Europe and Early Ming wares were the best examples available. Moreover the movement was orientated towards fine art which meant that it could easily degenerate into dilettantism. British pottery has always had an earthier more workman-like flavour, a heritage perhaps of the belief that pottery is for use, as has been the case from Medieval times right through early Staffordshire to the present day. We must accord some of this healthier influence to thinkers like John Ruskin, and William Morris and his followers. The latter's attitude to work and craftsmanship was heeded abroad rather than at home, but it was to have its effect here too, eventually. The Scandinavians learned early from Morris' views and were guided in their use of wood and metal, whilst it is a significant fact that the group of friends in Japan, under the late Dr. Yanagi, dedicated to seek the preservation of traditional craftsmanship in all fields, understood and appreciated William Morris' message.

Bernard Leach was and is of that group, and his life is central to the whole story of the revival as well as to what has happened since.

The early schools of art such as the Central School of Arts and Crafts opened by W. B. Lethaby and Sydney Cockerell, Morris' followers, and the Camberwell School of Art, were imbued at least in part by the spirit of fine craftsmanship. All too often though 'pottery' meant 'pottery decorating' on industrial white earthenware bodies, and only gradually did a real feeling for the material arise. But from these schools came many pioneer potters like Reginald Wells, W. B. Dalton, Charles Vyse, and eventually the fine artist potter William Staite Murray (1881–1962). William Staite Murray's attitude to clay was that it was an expressive medium capable, in the hands of a master, of standing comparison with the best of painting and sculpture. This point of view has helped to form one current of opinion that has remained with us ever since.

However, it is the vision, the work and the teaching (through his books and followers), of Bernard Leach that have given the pottery in this country its main stream. Bernard Leach and his first pupil Michael Cardew helped British potters to appreciate two main strengths; Far Eastern standards of perfection, and the directness and vigour of the pre-industrial peasant potter. Up to the time of the late war William Staite Murray, Bernard Leach and Michael Cardew with their respective students, apprentices and co-workers were, with a few exceptions, alone in this field of work. Yet they embodied even then attitudes of mind and methods of work that have influenced ever since those who came after them.

For some of these post-war potters, this 'influence' took the form of rejection in part or all, of the established opinion, and a new generation of potter/painters and potter/sculptors emerging after the first five years of post-war austerity, made some initial changes. For example, a spate of colourful, decorative earthenware followed, but this generally speaking did not last much beyond the middle fifties. (A notable exception can be seen in the maiolica of Alan Caiger-Smith.) What did endure and grow from this time, however, was the work of two remarkable potters Lucie Rie and Hans Coper. Lucie Rie with her exquisitely refined stoneware and porcelain, and Hans Coper with pots born from a highly original form sense, with their scumbled surfaces and monumental quality, brought something entirely new to the scene. Also more easily overlooked from this period because it built up more slowly and took place in the background was the re-emergence of the workshops based largely on Leach's conception of the small team working together in a co-operative venture to produce domestic ware at reasonable prices. It was fortunate indeed that this coincided with a gradual but steadily increasing rise in the affluence of our society and an equally slow, but nevertheless genuine, awakening of a sizeable minority to the fact that pottery made by hand by artist craftsmen had an appeal altogether different from its factory-made counterpart. Harry and May Davis near Camborne in Cornwall, Ray Finch at Winchcombe in Gloucestershire, Geoffrey Whiting at Droitwich, and others, as well as the Leach Pottery at St. Ives where both Bernard and his son David worked, were all either established or at least regenerated during this post-war period. In addition to this it was not long before a start was made by them on training the next generation of workshop potters. Those who are only now really becoming established.

As to the schools of art at this time, if their main contribution was in the field of education, not the least of their achievements was to enliven the general scene by the fostering of hand building methods such as coiling and slabbing which have given a much wider range in form and decoration to the whole world of pottery generally. The sixties have seen the main examination of these schools change from National Diploma in Design to Diploma in Art and Design with its broader syllabus. That there will be potters coming from these courses who will make a contribution to the pottery of this country is undoubtedly true, but what the accumulative effect of the change will be, remains to be seen in the next decade.

BIOGRAPHICAL NOTES TO THE POTTERS

ARBEID, Dan, Wendens Amber, Saffron Walden, Essex. Born London 1928. Began pottery in Beer-Sheba in 1956. Central School of Art, London. First exhibition Primavera London 1959. Makes individual and usually large pieces in stoneware. Exhibitions: Primavera, London 1959; Ceylon Tea Centre, London 1959; Boymans Museum, Rotterdam 1960; Guild of Applied Art, Bristol 1961; Prague 1961; National Museum of Wales 1961; Primavera 1963; Midland Group Gallery, Nottingham 1964; Kestner Museum, Hanover 1964; Molton Gallery, London; Oslo 1966. Work in Victoria & Albert Museum, Bristol Museum, Derby Museum, National Museum of Wales.

AULD, Ian, Emu Paddock, Grittleton, Chippenham, Essex. Born 1928. Studied painting before turning to pottery. Mainly makes slab built pots sometimes a heavy textured surface is achieved by application of a rough slip containing coarse fire-clay grog. Pots are all fired to stoneware in a reducing atmosphere using dry ash glazes. Work architectural sculptured in concept rather than functional. Has taught at Central School and Camberwell, London, now teaching at Bath Academy of Art. Exhibitions: Primavera, London 1961, 1966; Craft Centre 1964

BALDWIN, Gordon, 2 Willowbrook, Eton College, Windsor, Berks. Work is fired at 1,100° centigrade, techniques used being coiling, throwing, slabbing and press moulding. Interests lie in sculpture but producing large bowls, dishes, vases. Exhibitions: Ten Modern Potters, Abbots Hall 1965; One-man Thames Gallery, Eton 1966, and various mixed shows.

BARRON, Paul, Thornfield, Bentley, Farnham, Surrey. First studied pottery at Brighton School of Art under Norah Bradon, later at the Royal College of Art with Helen Pincombe. Potter in stoneware, formerly slipware, making largely individual pieces with a small amount of table ware. Regular exhibitor with the National Craft Societies. Work shown in Amsterdam, Prague, Tokyo, etc. Joint exhibition at C.P.A. with H. Hammond and others in May 1965. Senior lecturer in ceramics at Farnham School of Art, Surrey.

BATTERHAM, Richard, Durweston, Blandford Forum, Dorset. Worked at St. Ives in Leach Workshop. Makes high fired stoneware and porcelain.

BOSCEAN POTTERY, St. Just-in-Penwith, Cornwall. A small group of potters making a full range of domestic stoneware in oil-fired kiln.

BRIGLIN POTTERY, 22 Crawford Street, London, W.1. A team of potters under the directorship of Brigitta Appleby producing a large quantity of domestic ware and decorative individual pieces.

BUCKLAND, Michael, Green Dene Croft, East Horsley, Surrey. Began pottery in 1952, becoming a potter when he assisted Denis Moore at East Horsley who had been making pottery there for some years. Now main occupation. Most of the pots being thrown, but a certain amount of slabbing and coiling. Prefers stoneware, and using copper red, aubergine, ash and iron glazes he makes table ware and individual exhibition pieces. Exhibitions: C.P.A., London 1965; Primavera 'New Faces' 1965; Guildford House 1965; Chichester Museum 1966.

BURR, Graham, 7 Egerton Drive, Greenwich, London, S.E.10. Work is in stoneware, mainly individual pieces, but also a small production of domestic ware. Studied at Camberwell School of Art. Exhibitions: Craft Centre of Great Britain; the Craftsman Potters Association; the Northern Craft Centre, and various exhibitions abroad.

CAIGER-SMITH, Alan, The Pottery, Aldermaston, Berks. Specialises in painted tin-glaze earthenware and reduced lustreware. Large range of domestic tableware and ovenware and tiles, and also a number of individual and experimental pieces. Exhibitions: Primavere 1963 and 1964.

CARDEW, Michael. Born England, 1901. After early experience of pottery with Edwin Beer Fishley he worked with Bernard Leach for two years from 1923. He started making slipware and galena glazed earthenware at the old Winchcombe Pottery in Gloucestershire, which he acquired in 1926, later moving to Wenford Bridge in Cornwall in 1939. His work at this time recaptured the form and spirit of early English country slipware. Since 1942 except for brief visits to Wenford Bridge most of his work has been in Africa—Achimota, Vume and Nigeria where he was Pottery Officer to the Nigerian Government. No history of the craft of pottery can be complete unless it takes into account the work of Michael Cardew. His understanding and use of materials and appreciation of native traditions wherever met have made a major contribution.

CASS, Barbara, Arden Pottery, 56 High Street, Henley-in-Arden. Was born in Germany and studied sculpture in Berlin. Came to England in 1950 and started the York pottery in 1952, learning by experience. Began stoneware four years later and since moving to the Midlands has worked entirely in this medium. Specialises in big thrown pots and candle-holders for churches. Two London one-man shows 1960 and 1965. Numerous mixed exhibitions. Work bought by Victoria & Albert Museum, various churches and collectors here and abroad.

CASSON, Michael. Born 1925. First pots in 1945. Hornsey A.T.D. 1952. First workshop in Russell Square 1952–59 making tin glazed earthenware. Then to Prestwood with oxidised and reducing stoneware. Part-time and full-time teaching of all kinds 1946–64, when he gave up teaching except for visiting lecturer on Harrow Studio-pottery course. Present Chairman of the Craftsmen Potters Association of Great Britain. Exhibiting member of Crafts Centre, Designer Craftsmen, and member World Crafts Organisation. Exhibitions: one-man shows at Heals 1959; C.P.A. 1960 and 1964; Woollands, with wife, Sheila, 1965; Crafts Centre with Victor Margrie 1962. Prague (Gold Medallist) 1963, and in most major group exhibitions during the last ten years.

CASSON, Sheila. Born 1930. Trained at Hornsey School of Art 1946–51. N.D.D. pottery and lithography. 1952 A.T.D. Spent five years teaching. Potting spasmodically since 1955 in earthenware. 1962 changed to oxidised stoneware, and then to reduced stoneware. Exhibited with husband Michael at C.P.A. 1964, and Woollands in 1965. Concentrating mainly on production tableware.

CLARK, Kenneth, 26 Ellerdale Road, Hampstead, London, N.W.3. Trained at Slade and Central School of Art & Design. Has studio workshop in central London working with his wife Ann Wyn Reeves. At present much involved in design development, both as Industrial Consultant and for clients where coloured glazes and special bodies for individual techniques are needed. Author of Practical Pottery and Ceramics. Has carried out many designs in silver and other metals. Other work has ranged from majolica picture frame for a Braque painting to designing a presentation set of silver spoons. In 1966 a representative selection of work sent on a tour of New Zealand. Consultant and visitor to several art schools in connection with Dip.A.D. Ceramic Courses as well as part-time lecturer at Central School of Art and Design.

CLARKSON, Derek, The Poplars, Bacup, Lancs. Trained at Manchester College of Art, Burnley School of Art. Teaches at Stockport, Burnley and Bolton schools of art. Head of Ceramic Department, Stafford College of Art. Senior lecturer, Mather College of Education, Manchester. Mainly stoneware 1,300° fired by gas; heavy reduction. Enjoys working in traditional techniques including brush decoration, iron on ash glazes, or wax and double glazing, also cut and impressed decoration. Experimenting with various bodies. Exhibitions: represented Great Britain at Academy of International Ceramics, Geneva.

COLE, Walter V., Rye Pottery, Ferry Road, Rye, Sussex. Born London 1913. Trained pottery and sculpture under John Skeaping. 1930–36 Woolwich Polytechnic and Central School of Art. Assistant to Eric Kennington 1936–38. Reopened pottery at Rye in 1947 (which had been closed during war years). Various pre-war exhibitions, member of old London Group. Work purchased by Contemporary Art Society. 1962 Silver medallist at International Ceramic Exhibition in Prague. 1966 Design Award London Design Centre. Exhibits yearly at Rye Society of Arts Summer Exhibition.

CONSTANTINIDES, Joanna, 2 Bells Chase, Great Baddow, Chelmsford, Essex. Mainly stoneware, some porcelain. Work sent through British Craft Export Group to Sydney, Tokyo and to the International

Ceramics Exhibition in Prague (Gold Medal award). Exhibitions: Munich, C.P.A., Spring 1965; East Anglia Crafts at Primavera, Spring 1967.

COOPER, Waistel, Culbone Lodge, Porlock, Somerset. Born 1921 in Ayr. Studied painting at Edinburgh College of Art. In 1946 went to Iceland to carry out some portrait commissions and stayed five years. In 1948 he began potting, and returned to Britain and established his studio in Porlock. In 1957 moved to Culbone. He makes high-temperature stoneware, decorated with wood ash glazes and metal oxides. All the pieces are individually designed. Fires in an oil-fired kiln and uses wood to induce reduction atmosphere. Exhibitions: Reykjavik; Heal & Son; Primavera; Arnolfini Gallery, Bristol; Scottish Craft Centre; Duoverton Art Gallery, and Taunton.

COPER, Hans. Born 1920. Began working in ceramics in 1947. Has contributed to many international exhibitions and periodically at Berkeley Galleries, London. Has work in Victoria & Albert Museum; Museum of Modern Art, New York; Stedelijk Museum, Amsterdam; Museum, Boymans—Van Beuningen, Rotterdam. Also in Stockholm, Tokyo, Melbourne, Toronto, Zurich.

DAN, John, Wivenhoe Pottery, High Street, Wivenhoe, Essex. Mainly fairly large stoneware pieces, recently some of them more like sculpture than pottery insofar as they are not always vessels.

DUCKWORTH, Ruth, c/o Mrs. E. Windmuller, Vicarage Court, Vicarage Gate, London, W.8. Produces stoneware and porcelain, mostly hand-built. The stoneware is mostly big and heavily grogged, the porcelain is small and sometimes very delicate. Exhibitions: Primavera 1960, 1962; Arnolfini Gallery, Bristol 1964; Craft Centre of Great Britain 1964; Renaissance Society, University of Chicago 1965; Craftsmen's Gallery, Chicago 1965; Gallery Mid-North, Chicago 1966; Matsuya Department Store, Tokyo 1967.

EELES, David, Shepherd's Well Pottery, Mosterton, Beaminster, Dorset. Prefers making mainly functional ware now for some fifteen years and believes that only with considerable repetition can one perfect a shape that is complete in itself. Specialises in tableware and ovenware in reduced stoneware and porcelain in an oil-fired kiln and oxidised earthenware. Exhibitions: Craftsmen's Potters Association, London; Craft Centre of Great Britain; Bluecoat Display Centre, Liverpool; permanent exhibition at Retreat Gallery, Burton Bradstock, Bridport, Dorset. Has undertaken various large murals in tin glazed earthenware, and salt glazed stoneware for London County Council and Caltex Oil Co., etc.

EMMS, Derek, 16 Bracken Close, Copeland Park Estate, Tittenson, Staffs. Born 1929. Studied at Accrington and Burnley Schools of Art before taking Art Teachers Diploma at Leeds College of Art. Originally trained in textile design but changed to pottery. On completion of National Service worked at the Leach Pottery, St. Ives. Since 1955 full-time lecturer at Stoke-on-Trent College of Art. Specialises in high-temperature reduced stoneware, and particularly interested in glaze experiments with simple natural materials. Exhibitions: Keele University 1964; Northern Crafts Centre, Accrington Museum & Art Gallery 1964; Robert John Gallery, Stoke on Trent 1965; Crafts Centre of Great Britain 1966.

FIELDHOUSE, Murray, Northfield Studio, Northfield, Tring, Herts. Born 1925. After long awaited demob from R.A.F., 1945, decided to be a craftsman in a community. 1946–47 worked with Harry Davis (still the potter he most admires). 1947–48 worked at Kingwood Design and Craftsmanship (Lester Campion, Ray Marshall, Mary Gibson Horrocks, Reginald Ampousah and briefly Michael Cardew all contributed). 1948 joined Pendley Centre of Adult Education. 1949 first Catalogue of twenty-one tableware shapes. 1950 joined by the late John Chappell. After illness 1952–54 courses established at Pendley to introduce pottery teachers to professional hand potters. 1954 Pottery Quarterly issued—appeared regularly for seven years—the potters forum. 1958 a second quarterly—'Crafts Review' started but hopes dashed a year later by strike. 1962–67 a little teaching, a little potting and travelling. Ambition—to make only medium sized bowls and edit an Encyclopaedia of Studio Potting. Has always maintained that the craftsman should and can look after their own affairs.

FINCH, Raymond, Winchcombe Pottery Ltd., Winchcombe, Gloucestershire. Ray Finch with a team of four produces at Winchcombe Pottery a wide range of domestic stoneware; almost the entire production is repetitive table and ovenware in rust, black and rust or semi matt white glazes.

FOURNIER, Robert, Castle Hill Cottages, Brenchley, Kent. Trained at Central School 1946–47, becoming technical assistant, and assistant to Miss Billington. Set up Ducketts Wood Pottery in 1947 making earthenware, mainly slipware. Attained subtle greys and blues by using tin glaze over slips. Mosaics and tilework mid 1950s. Set up stoneware kiln in Greenwich in 1962 and moved to present pottery at Castle Hill in 1965. Oxidised stonewares with some original glazes. Handbuilt work since 1964—slab, thumb pots, etc. but basic output still coffee services, kitchen ware, etc. Good deal of lecturing and teaching.

FUCHS, Annette Rose, The Old School House, Highmoor, Near Henley-on-Thames, Oxon. Started pottery training at the Royal Salford Technical College School of Art, then two years at Camberwell School of Art after which worked at the Briglin Pottery before joining sister in her pottery in London. Now at Henley on her own. Has specialised in earthenware concentrating on getting pleasantly coloured and textured glazes. Mostly practical ware but some decorative bottles and slab pots. Pottery decorated with applied clay, sgraffito and wax resist. Marked ARF.

FUCHS, Tessa, 21 Great Western Road, London, W.9. Worked in London for six years and had several exhibitions. One-man show at Bluecoat Display Centre, Liverpool 1966, having previously had a show with sister Annette at the Craftsmen Potters Shop. Pots are earthenware of a rather decorative type, the most characteristic being thinly thrown and decorated with sgraffito through a jewel-like turquoise or tin glaze on to oxide. Also uses inlaid glazes and simplified plant and animal motifs. Does practical ware (coffee, fruit and punch sets) and also individual pieces of large platters and bowls, and in particular animal forms with applied clay embellishments and terracotta figures.

GREEN, Alan Spencer, The Old Corn Mill, Wimbish, Saffron Waldon, Essex. Works in fine stoneware and porcelain and is particularly interested in glazes. All his pieces are hand thrown and individual in nature, no sets and no 'repeats' being made. Took part in the international competition for potters under age of 45 in Marseille in 1965, and his complete entry of four pots was bought by the Musee Cantini. Won gold medal at the International Exhibition Faenza in the same year. In 1966 was chosen to take part in the exhibition 'Modern European Pottery' organised by John Sparks. Specialises in Oriental ceramics.

GREENWOOD, Pamela, Manoir Saint Leger, Ouilly-du-houley, 14 Moyaux, France. Trained at the Camberwell Art School, and spent one year at the Leach Pottery in St. Ives and then to a small pottery workshop in Normandy (France).

GRIFFITHS, Arthur J., White House, Walton-le-Wolds, Loughborough, Leics. Is running a Dip.A.D. course in Ceramics, and has his own workshop. Trained with Harris Davis and very interested in tableware production. All the work is in stoneware, in a wide range including garden pottery and plant containers, as well as individual work for exhibitions. Exhibited abroad as well as in Great Britain including a shared show at Derby Art Gallery. Also exhibited at the Craftsmen Potters Shop, Northern Crafts Centre, and Midland Group Gallery, Nottingham which has a permanent show on his pots.

HAMMOND, Henry, Staceys Flat, Bentley, Farnham, Surrey.

HANSSEN, Gwyn, Les Grandes Fougeres, Acheres, Henrichemont 18, France or Farnham School of Art, Farnham. Born 1935. Trained with Ivan McMeekin, Sturt Pottery, Mittagong, Australia. Later Winchcombe Pottery, Glos. with Raymond Finch, and Leach Pottery, St. Ives. Started own workshop in 1960 in London, making domestic stoneware, mainly for kitchen use. 1964 worked at Wenford Bridge Pottery (by kind permission of Michael Cardew) making wood-fired domestic stoneware. 1967 establishing stoneware workshop in France making wood-fired domestic wares. Exhibitions: Primavera 1962, 1964, 1966. Canada 'British Potters', and Molton Gallery 1965 'British Potters'.

HANSSEN, Louis, 4 Redcliffe Gardens, London, S.W.10. Has made a range of oxidised domestic stoneware as well as large individual and sculptural pieces.

HORLOCK-STRINGER, Harry, Taggs Yard School of Ceramics, 11½ Woodlands Road, Barnet, London, S.W.13. Originally Fulham Studio Pottery, now at Taggs Yard. Produces mainly red earthenware well vitrified at plus 1,120°, using a Lead-Borate Tin Glaze over slips, producing speckled brown, speckled green, and blue effects with spriggs. Mostly useful wares and sprigged com-

6

memorative wares, also ceramic sculpture in oxidised stoneware. Now moving towards simpler, unsprigged work exposing vitrified body. Exhibitions: Tokyo, Paris, Prague, London and Provinces. Work in British Museum.

HOY, Anita, 50 Julian Avenue, London, W.3. Attended Copenhagen School of Art 1933–1937, then joined Hooelbaek Stoneware Factory, subsequently Natalie Krebs at Saxbo. Returned to England in 1939 and joined Bullers Ltd. at Stoke, starting a studio department, working with the factory's porcelain and high-temperature reducing glazes. In 1952 joined Royal Doulton as designer for salt glazed stoneware at Lambeth. Has been making porcelain and stoneware in own studio since 1957. Teaches also at Farnham School of Art and Hammersmith and also at Richmond. Exhibited at C.P.A. in 1961.

KELLAM, Colin, c/o Shinners Bridge Pottery, Dartington, S. Devon. Born 1942. Trained at Loughborough College of Art 1959–63 NDD. 1963 experience in moulding department of Hathern Pottery Ltd. 1963 went to work for Marianne de Trey. 1967 still connected with Shinners Bridge but working alone with wood-fired kiln. Domestic, architectural projects, fountains, etc.

LEACH, Bernard, C.B.E. Born 1887 in Hong Kong. After school in England, completing his studies at the Slade School of Art, he returned to the Far East to teach in 1909. On coming back to this country in 1920 he set up the Leach Pottery at St. Ives, Cornwall. His national and international exhibitions and awards are far too numerous to list. His has been the major single influence on the rebirth of craft pottery in this country if not throughout the world.

LEACH, David, Lowerdown Pottery, Bovey Tracey, Devon. Has been potting professionally and continuously for some thirty-six years, since joining his father, Bernard Leach, in 1930. After twenty-five years working in close collaboration with him as student, manager and then partner, he decided to start his own pottery in Bovey Tracey in 1956. Has built his own large oil-fired stoneware kiln, and made thrown stoneware and translucent porcelain, chiefly functional, developing many of the techniques of body and glaze he started at the Leach Pottery. Is assisted by his two sons John and Jeremy. Has taught at Loughborough, Harrow, Bournemouth, Poole, Exeter and Farnham Colleges of Art. Vice-chairman of the Craftsmen Potters', Association. Examples of his work are in the Victoria and Albert Museum and other national collections.

LEACH, Janet, St. Ives Pottery, St. Ives, Cornwall. Established her own pottery at Threefold Farm, Spring Valley, N.Y. in 1947, and later went to Japan for two years to study pottery under auspices of Bernard Leach and Shoji Hamada. In 1956 came to England to marry Bernard Leach and now works with him in the management of the Leach Pottery. Born in Texas 1918. Moved to New York in 1937 to continue art studies and worked as a sculptor's assistant on a Federal art project. In 1947 studied pottery at the Indwood Pottery and at Alfred University. Exhibitions at Takumi Craft Shop, Osaka 1955, Primavera 1960, Contemporary English Potters, Boymann's Museum, Rotterdam 1961. Examples of her work in Boymann's Museum, Bristol Museum, Cardiff Museum of Art, Stoke-on-Trent School of Art, Victoria & Albert Museum, Newark Museum of Art.

LELIVA, Trentham de, 6 Hanover Street, Brighton, Sussex. Producing a range of oxidised domestic stoneware and large individual pieces.

LEWENSTEIN, Eileen, 5 Belsize Lane, London, N.W.5. Founded Briglin Pottery with Brigitta Appleby in 1948. Since 1959 has worked as an individual potter mainly in stoneware. Primarily interested in the construction of clay shapes by any possible method, but occasionally enjoys throwing. At present making ceramic screens. Exhibitions: Eva Hauser Gallery 1960, 1963, 1966; C.P.A. 1961; Crafts Centre 1962; International Ceramics Exhibition, Prague 1962; Craftsmanship Today 1965; Clay and Walls, Whitechapel 1965. Lecturer Hornsey College of Art, Vice-Chairman Craftsmen Potters Association.

LOWNDES, Gillian, Emy Paddock, Crittleton, Chippenham, Wilts. Born 1936. Studied pottery at Central School of Arts and Crafts. Pots mainly coiled or slab-built with soft slabs of clay. More concerned with form rather than function. Works in oxidised stoneware in an electric kiln using mainly ash on opacified glazes. Often double glazing to produce rich quality. Teaching at West of England College of Art and Harrow School of Arts and Crafts. Exhibitions: Bristol Guild of Applied Arts 1963; Primavera 1965 and 1966.

MALTBY, John, Stoneshill Pottery, Stoneshill, Crediton, Devon. Born 1936. Studied sculpture for four years at Leicester College of Art. In 1962 gave up full-time teaching to work with David Leach at Lowerdown, and in 1965 started own pottery at Stoneshill making a wide range of domestic oxidised stoneware and some individual pieces including coffee and tea sets, casseroles, etc.

MARGRIE, Victor, Red House, Hempstead Lane, Potten End, Berkhamstead. Work has until recently been domestic oxydised stoneware although not of a repetitive kind, rather a series of projects re-appraising traditional function and purpose. White pots have always been of special interest and white glazes predominate. Sprigging, incising or slip inlay is the usual form of decoration, never painting. Exhibited at many mixed shows, including Artist Craftsmen Exhibition at Camden Arts Centre. Participated in the two Two-man shows at Crafts Centre. In 1963 founded, with Michael Casson, the Harrow Studio Pottery Course. Member C.O.I.D. Studio Pottery Selection Committee.

MARLOW, Reginald. Specialises in studio pottery, particularly stoneware. Recent exhibitions include Design Centre, Northern Crafts Centre, and Hanley Art Gallery. President of the Society of Designer Craftsmen, Chairman of the Red Rose Guild of Designer Craftsmen.

MARSHALL, Ray, Bridgefoot Pottery, Stedham, Midhurst. The potter works alone on the outskirts of Stedham overlooking the river Rother. He makes stoneware using either wood ash or felspathic glazes and fires between 1,250° and 1,300° C. Regulation lines consist of tea or coffee sets, fruit sets, jugs as well as individual pieces, drawing his inspiration mainly from the ancient middle east. Decorated usually by impressing and combing the wet clay.

MARSHALL, William, Leach Pottery, St. Ives. Born 1923, and was first apprentice to be employed at the Leach Pottery. He started there in 1938 and has remained there since. His work has been included in various exhibitions, including with Bernard Leach at Liberty's, London 1956; with Janet Leach at Primavera, London 1959, and at the Boymann Museum, Rotterdam, Arts Council Travelling Exhibitions, and others. Is member of the Penwith Society of Arts, Midland Group of Artists, Nottingham, 1966, and Craft Centre of Great Britain, London 1966.

METCALFE, Paul H., Pottery Cottage, Dunkirk, Faversham, Kent. Trained as a technical assistant at the Pottery Department at Farnham School of Art. Opened own studio at Westbourne Grove in 1965. Makes mainly tableware and tall individual bottles in oxidised stoneware. Works on theme of contrasting glazed surfaces with unglazed portions, placing emphasis on relating negative curves with positive shapes. In 1965 was awarded Diploma of Honour at International Exhibition of Ceramics in Geneva where the theme was 'glazes'.

MOORE, Denis, Green Dene Croft, East Horsley, Surrey. Worked for over twenty years in high-fired stoneware. Uses raw materials (clays, sands and ashes) from the terrain in his pottery at East Horsley. Has developed wide palette of glaze colours, specialising in the rouge flambes from copper, viz: sang de boeuf (crimrose) and aubergine (purple). Uses open-fired kiln, fuelled with wood and oil. Exhibitions: C.P.A., London 1964, 1965; Primavera 1965; Guilford House 1965; Chichester City Museum 1966, and various abroad. Articles for Studio International, Le Combat, Paris, and Arts Review.

NEWMAN, Bryan, Halls Farm, Aller, Langport, Somerset. Produces reduced stoneware at 1,300°. Wide range of work from coffee sets—coil pots. Slab pots to abstract sculpture and tile panels. Exhibitions: Copenhagen, Munich, Tokyo, Brussels, Geneva.

NISBET, Eileen. Studied at Central School of Art and Design. Has taught subsequently at Harrow and Central Schools of Art and Design. Exhibited at Tea Centre Exhibition with Harrow School; Crafts Council of Great Britain, Piccadilly; Whitechapel Gallery 'Clay and Walls'; Mural work for Buckinghamshire County Council 1966. Concentrates mainly on large dishes and ceramic murals.

PEARSON, Colin, The Quay Pottery, High Street, Aylesford, Maidstone, Kent. Born 1923. After service with R.A.F. studied painting at Goldsmiths. Following brief spell of teaching became student with Ray Finch at Winchcombe and later assistant to David Leach at Aylesford Pottery taking over when he left. Own workshop begun in 1962 at Aylesford. Exhibitions: C.P.A. 1963; shared 1964 Crafts Centre Exhibition with Ian Auld. Participated in various mixed shows. Work in various public and private collections. Silver medal at Geneva 1965. Member of Crafts Centre, Red

Rose Guild. Council member of C.P.A. Teaches at Camberwell School of Art and is visiting tutor to the Harrow Studio Pottery Course.

PINCOMBE, Helen, The Forge, Steel's Lane, Oxshott, Surrey. Born India 1908. Educated in Australia. Training: Central School of Art and Craft, Royal College of Art. Teaching till early fifties, own studio since 1949—first part-time, later full-time. Exhibitions at Primavera and work shown at various exhibitions at home and abroad. Work in various Museums at home and abroad.

PLAHN, Gordon, Langton Pottery, Langton Green, Tunbridge Wells, Kent. First workshop in Sevenoaks in 1958 for three years. Then to Langton Green in an old blacksmith's house, shop and smithy. Produces mostly tableware such as coffee sets, mugs, etc. in stoneware. Makes some individual pieces. Has had a one-man exhibition of individual work in Tunbridge Wells in 1964.

PLEYDELL-BOUVERIE, Katherine, Kilmington Manor, Near Warminster, Wilts. Born 1895. Trained at Central School and St. Ives Pottery. Produced stoneware at Coleshill 1925–1940, specialised in wood ash glazes in wood fuel kiln at 1,250°–1,400° in reduced oxidised atmosphere. At Kilmington since 1950, specialises mainly in pots and bowls for flowers at middle temperature in oxidising temperature. Latest exhibition: Spring 1965 at C.P.A., 3 Lowndes Court, London, W.1.

PLOWMAN, Thomas, Stalham Pottery, High Street, Stalham, Norfolk. Runs Stalham Pottery on a full-time basis producing stoneware pottery of a consistently high standard of design. Emphasis on production of thrown pots, but workshop is geared to a flexible approach. Work includes individual pieces, exhibition work and a wide range of standard domestic items which are on show in a spacious shop. Exhibitions include one-man shows at Craftsmen Potters Association 1963; Edinburgh Festival 1965, and other exhibitions in Great Britain and overseas.

REEVE, John, Longlands Pottery, Hennock, Newton Abbot, S. Devon. Born Ontario, Canada 1929. Does stoneware and porcelain fire cone 8 to 12, two-chamber, oil-fired, natural draft, climbing downdraught kiln. Exhibited at Primavera and recently (1966) at University of Minnesota, U.S.A.

REEVES, Ann Wynn, 26 Ellerdale Road, Hampstead, London, N.W.3. Trained at Willesden School of Art and in Ceramic Department of Central School of Art and Design. Married to Kenneth Clark and shares studio in Central London. Much involved in architectural ceramics including murals in collaboration with husband. Has also designed many of the decorated tiles and other ware produced by Kenneth Clark pottery. Has exhibited little in recent years due to increasing commissions. Pieces in the Victoria & Albert Museum as well as other museums in U.K. and abroad. Was one of the seven English potters chosen for International Ceramic Exhibition in Tokyo 1965.

RIE, Lucie. Born in Vienna in 1902, trained at Arts and Crafts there, and then worked in own workshop for a few years. Came to London in 1938 and opened workshop there in 1939. Exhibited at Paris, Monza, Brussels, Triennale Milan, Amsterdam, Rotterdam, Goteborg, New York, Minnesota and Munich. Several exhibitions with Hans Coper at Berkeley Galleries and two one-man exhibitions. Pots in the following collections: Victoria & Albert Museum; Museum Modern Art New York; and in various continental and Commonwealth museums.

ROOKE, Bernard, 9 Guildford Grove, London, S.E.10. Produces individual pottery, but main bulk of his work is concerned with ceramics as applied to interior and exterior design. Has done many commissions of murals, fountains, sculptures, and lamp-bases. Exhibitions: London, Sweden, Germany, Australia, Denmark. Extensive sales in U.S.A.

SHOTTON, Margaret, Cross Lane Pottery, Byfield, Rugby (on B.4036 between Banbury and Daventry). Produces mainly a range of thrown tableware in oxidised stoneware with some impressed or applied decoration and with ash and feldspathic glazes, generally used one over the other. Also individual slab-built plant troughs, boxes, etc. with carved, impressed and applied decoration and fired to stoneware. Exhibitions: Crafts Centre, London 1964, 1965; Ceylon Tea Centre, London 1965; Crafts Exhibition, Banbury 1965; Crafts Council, Coventry and Shrewsbury 1966; Hampstead Artists Council, Artist Craftsmen 1966.

SOLLY, John, F.R.S.A., 36 London Road, Maidstone, Kent. Born Maidstone 1928. Trained at Maidstone, Stoke-on-Trent, L.C.C. Central School, and Camberwell. Spent short time at Rye Pottery and Winchcombe. Set up own workshop in 1952 producing high-fired domestic earthenware and more recently (1964) included oven-proof pots. Makes all types and is running summer pottery courses since 1960, and teaching part-time at Harrow and Tunbridge Wells. Two one-man exhibitions at C.P.A., Lowndes Court 1961 and 1963.

TREY, Marianne de, Shinners Bridge Pottery, Dartington, Totnes, S. Devon. Has worked at Shinners Bridge pottery since 1938, producing mostly oxidised stoneware for the table and a series of shapes for flower arranging. Personal work includes porcelain, slab-built bottles and a variety of pots fired in a wood kiln built by Colin Kellam. One of three assistants who is now producing work on his own. One-man exhibitions at Primavera and the Crafts Centre.

WALLWORK, Alan, Greenwich Studios, 19 Blackheath Road, London, S.E.10. Uses combinations of techniques mainly coiled and slabbing, throwing when a symmetrical section is required. Methods of making and decoration are chosen which involve dramatic manipulation of clay surfaces contrasted with glazes. Does mainly non-repetitive work with exception of certain standard items—mainly tiles. Most pieces have a functional aspect.

WHITING, Geoffrey, Avoncroft Pottery, Hampton Lovett, Droit-wich, Worcs. Basic production of domestic stoneware, supplemented by more individual work in stoneware and hard porcelain. Held fifth exhibition in 1966 at Craftsmen Potters Association. Has had work purchased by some fifteen public collections at home and overseas and is represented in two permanent British Council Travelling Exhibitions of the work of British Artist Potters.

THALMESSINGER, Anne, The Retreat, Sandhurst Road, Yeteley, Camberley. During the last seven years has produced earthenware firing at 1,120°–1,200° C. Has now installed a gas kiln and will concentrate on stoneware. Has experimented on variety of techniques and methods.

WREN, Denise K., The Oxshott Pottery, Potter's Croft, Oakshade Road, Oxshott, Surrey. Born in Western Australia, studied at Kingston on Thames School of Art under Archibald Knox. Special interest in Celtic and Early English pottery. Specialises in wheel-thrown and hand-built pitcher, upright goblet and bottle shapes, designed chiefly for floral arrangements, in high-fire colour and salt-glazed stoneware, sometimes with designs and rough deep scorings, with cobalt, ochre and rutile oxides rubbed in, fired in high-fire coke and gas kilns. Each piece is an individual one. Exhibitions: Berkeley Galleries, London; Prague (Silver medal); Tokyo; Auckland; Sydney; etc.

WREN, Rosemary D., The Oxshott Pottery, Potters' Croft, Oakshade Road, Oxshott, Surrey. Makes individual stoneware pieces only, using various techniques. Some thrown pots but mostly simplified animal and bird forms, built up hollow from flattened coils, three inches to three feet high. Pots frequently salt glazed, ceramic sculptures usually stained with oxides, unglazed, but fired to a sheet in reducing atmosphere in gas or coke kiln. Exhibitions in many world capitals and has had five one-man shows in London. Pieces in the Victoria & Albert Museum, Stuttgart, etc. Gold Medal, Prague International 1962.

SECTION ONE

HAND BUILDING

SECTION ONE

HAND BUILDING

CLAY-LIKE FORM, interesting surface treatment, and colour derived from clays and glazes fused by heat, are common qualities shared by all the best pottery whether made with or without the aid of the wheel. The differences between the two methods of making pots become apparent when the techniques involved are considered in more detail. Building pots by hand, the most ancient method stemming from Neolithic times if not beyond, is an obviously slower way than that of using the wheel. This time factor is vital. The technique in essence is that of using smaller pieces of clay in the form of coils, strips, pads, or slabs pressed flat or into moulds, to form the whole pot by joining up these parts in various ways. Only in the hand building process of 'pinching', usually smaller shapes, is the total amount of clay of which the pot is to be made used at one and the same time, and this is really like a very slow rotatory action. Most hand builder-potters today employ a variety of methods often on the same pot; see the work of Gordon Baldwin for example.

The qualities one looks for in hand built forms are not quite the same as those one hopes to find in 'thrown' pottery. Because of the slower pace of making, and more varied building techniques, a greater and far more sculptural range of forms is possible. Size alone is no bar. Monumentality, not necessarily always associated just with size, but often arising from it, is one quality that comes to mind with the best of this work. Ian Auld's slab bottles seem to have this almost inevitable stature. Surface quality is another. The very way that the pot is built up means that the surface is continually being altered. In coiling the coils can either remain to form an integral part of the pot form, or be scumbled away leaving a texture of varying degrees of complexity. In either case the treatment leaves its mark. In slabbing, clay is pressed into sheets before being luted together. The way it is pressed and cut, as well as the surface it is pressed on or into, can dictate the final result. Scoring, incising, slip inlaying, rubbing-in of oxides, pouring of glazes, and many other devices are employed by hand builders to enliven the surface quality in order to enhance the overall form of their work. More elaborate form structures together with more agitated surfaces seem to constitute one growing attitude to non-wheel made pottery. The simple, beautifully made, hand built pottery of Helen Pincombe, or the rugged more quickly cut forms of Janet Leach and John Reeve represent a rather different view.

In general, though, all potters see the tremendous potential in hand built pottery, and most production potters of domestic tableware take the opportunity to explore other avenues of form by this most expressive medium. Alan Wallwork is in fact one workshop potter who has made it his first method of production.

The schools can encourage their students to experiment whilst, one hopes, giving them a sound basis of craftsmanship. Clay, glaze, and fire, form, colour and texture, are as always still the ingredients the potter has to manipulate.

The wide range of expression achieved by the potters of this country has not yet led to the wild excesses seen in some parts of the world. It will be a challenge to hold onto the traditional strengths whilst exploring new fields with a creative imagination.

Hans Coper

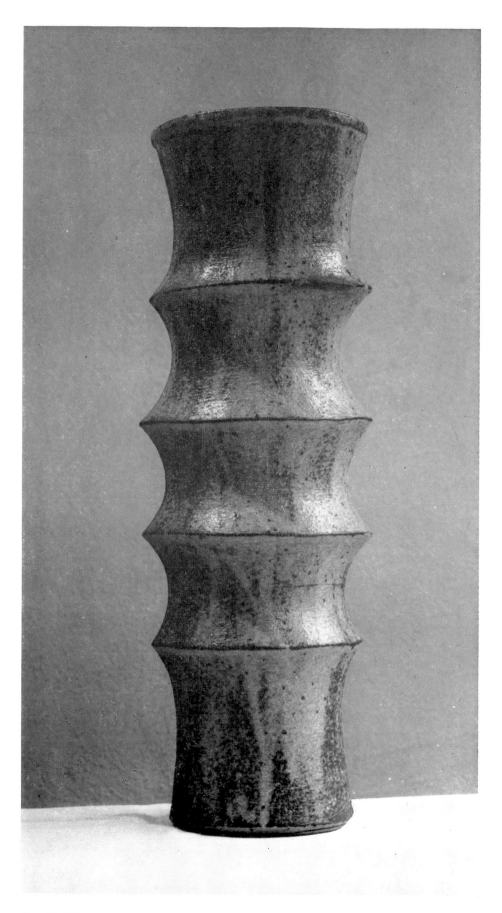

Dan Arbeid/1
Tall coiled five-section pot, yellow green ash glaze breaking to rust red. 20″ high. 1300 °C reduction, oil-fired

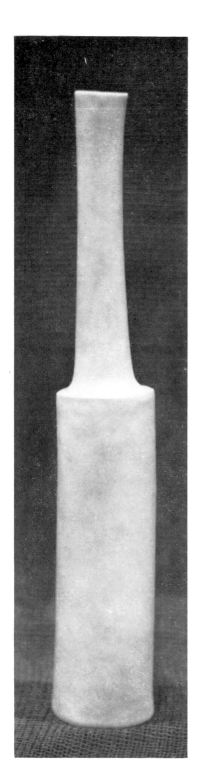

Dan Arbeid/2
Proto-porcelain bottle semi matt grey white glaze. 18″ high. 1300°C reduction, oil fired.

Ian Auld/3
Large coiled stoneware pots incised decoration, poured ash glaze. 22″ high.

Ian Auld/4
Slab-built stoneware bottle with coiled top ; applied grogged slip. Surface incised and impressed. Dry buff glaze reduced 1300°C. 20″ high.

Ian Auld/5
Slab-built stoneware dish combed decoration. Titanium and dolomite cream coloured glaze. 1300°C reduction. 15″ × 12″.

Ian Auld/6
Slab-built stoneware pot coiled top, relief and combed decoration. Thin matt ochre coloured glaze, reduced firing 1300°C. 17″ high.

Gordon Baldwin/7
Large thrown and slabbed pot. High-fired earthenware, white and orange with black specles. 4' high.

Gordon Baldwin/8
Part thrown part slab-built high-fired earthenware pot. Red clay with matt green glaze. 30" high.

Gordon Baldwin/9
Coiled earthenware pot, with combing. Buff black and green glazed. 1100°C. 20″ high.

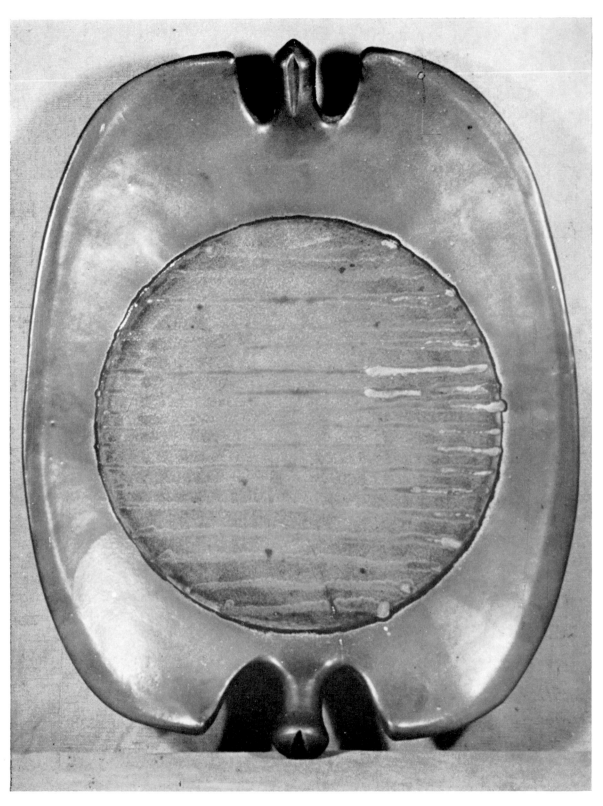

Gordon Baldwin/10
Pressed and thrown dish. Bronze black with blue centre. High-fired earthenware. 18″ wide.

Gordon Baldwin/11
High-fired earthenware hand built pinched dish with combed decoration. Inside bright blue and green. 12″ wide.

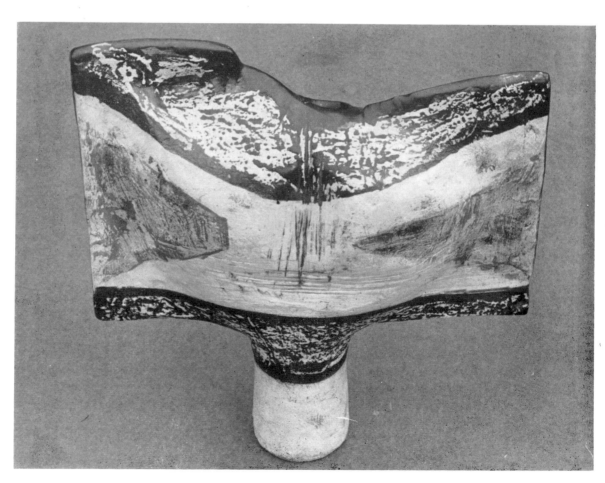

Gordon Baldwin/12
Coiled and slabbed high-fired earthenware pot. Black, white and blue. 15″ high.

Gordon Baldwin/13
Large thrown and slabbed high-fired earthenware pot. Buff clay speckled with black brown and green overtones. 24″ high.

Briglin/14
Slab-built earthenware pot with six spouts,
red body and dark brown glaze.

Briglin/15
Hand built earthenware pot in red clay
with black glazed centre.

Graham Burr/16
Group of stoneware slab-built pots. Double curved pot in dipped and poured glazes, 12½″×11⅛″. Rectangular pot with glazed areas 13¾″×11¼″. Small slab pot with low relief decoration, 5½″ high×3¾″. 1280°C oxidised.

Graham Burr/17
Slab-built stoneware with cut-out fluted clay facade, dry and smooth pale ash glazes. 10½″ high.

Derek Clarkson/18
Earthenware coiled pot with broken-brown pigment on unglazed body. Yellow
and blue-black pooled glazes in cupheads. 1170°C.

Waistel Cooper/19
Tall oxidised stoneware bottle with stopper.
Thrown and added pieces with textured surface.

John Dan/20
Stoneware hand built pot with inlaid white vitreous slip. 18½" high.

Ruth Duckworth/21
Coiled stoneware pot, grey clay, grey-green glaze. 14" high.

Ruth Duckworth/22
Porcelain pot with reduced copper red glaze. 6″ high.

Ruth Duckworth/23
Porcelain form, ochre and
matt porcelain glaze. 9″ high.

Ruth Duckworth/24
Porcelain pot with reduced copper red glaze. 11″ high.

Ruth Duckworth/25
Coiled stoneware pot, grogged surface and applied copper and iron. Matt ash glaze. 22" high.

Ruth Duckworth/26
Coiled stoneware pot. Clay with copper matt glaze, showing turquoise. 12" high

Robert Fournier/27
Pinched pebble form, oxidised stoneware pot with poured glaze over textured surface. 10″ diameter.

Pamela Greenwood/28
Pressed stoneware dish with bird decoration, brown and white surface, colours on coarse body. 14″ diameter

Arthur Griffiths/29
Grogged porcelain pot with copper rubbed
into textured surface. 9″ high.

Arthur Griffiths/30
Large hand built stoneware pot with incised
and inlaid lines. 17″ high.

Louis Hanssen/31
Large stoneware jar, dark body with
white glaze breaking to red
where clay shows through.

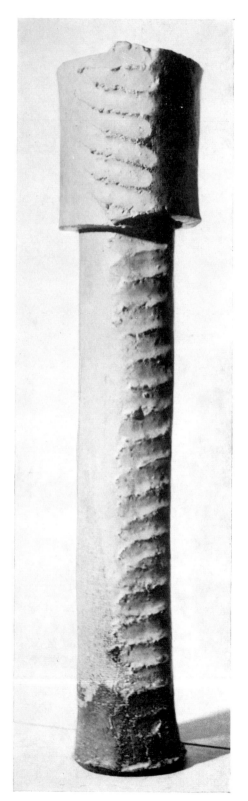

Louis Hanssen/32
Tall oxidised stoneware 'wrap-round'.
pot with rough joined seam.
Approx. 24″ high,

Louis Hanssen/33
Large oxidised stoneware bottle with
textured surface and splashed glaze.

Louis Hanssen/34
Oxidised stoneware pot with seam.
Top dipped in oxidised iron glaze.

Colin Kellam/35
Slab-built stoneware pot,
reduced wood-fired ash and
iron glaze. 12″ high.

Colin Kellam/36
Large slab-built stoneware pot,
wood-fired ash iron glaze.
42″×24″×15″. Small slab pot 6″ high.

F

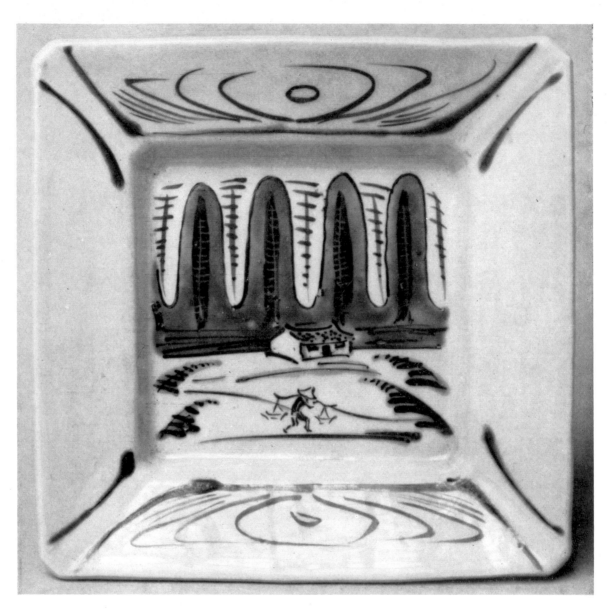

Bernard Leach/37
Enamelled porcelain dish made in Japan. 6″ square.

Janet Leach/38
Slab-built stoneware pot with ash glaze. 10″ high.

Eileen Lewenstein/39
'Wrap-round' stoneware pot with rich
poured mat and semi-matt glazes. 10" high.

Eileen Lewenstein/40
Large coiled stoneware pot
with copper brushed on outside,
glazed inside. 18" high.

Gillian Lowndes/41
Group of coiled oxidised stoneware pots with thin matt glazes.

Gillian Lowndes/42
Three hand built stoneware pots with dark brown and white matt glazes

Bryan Newman/43
Oxidised stoneware form 6″ high

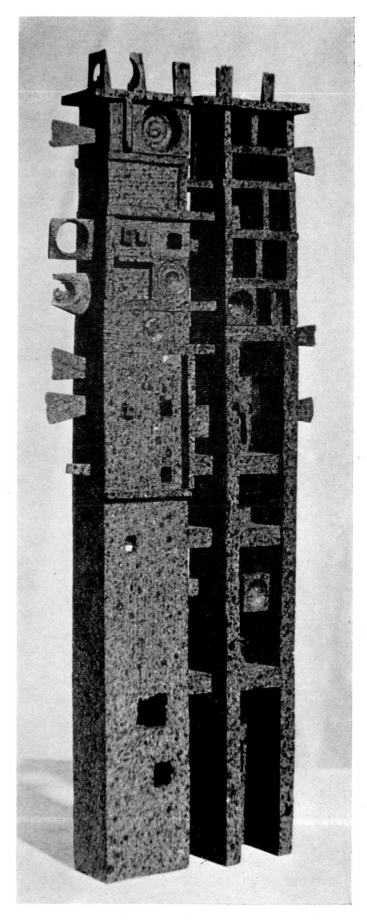

Bryan Newman/44
Oxidised stoneware form
with mangansee oxide in the clay body,
unglazed. 20″ high.

Bryan Newman/45
Oxidised stoneware form made up of parts of pots, manganese pigment applied then copper and
zirconium pigment. 10″ high.

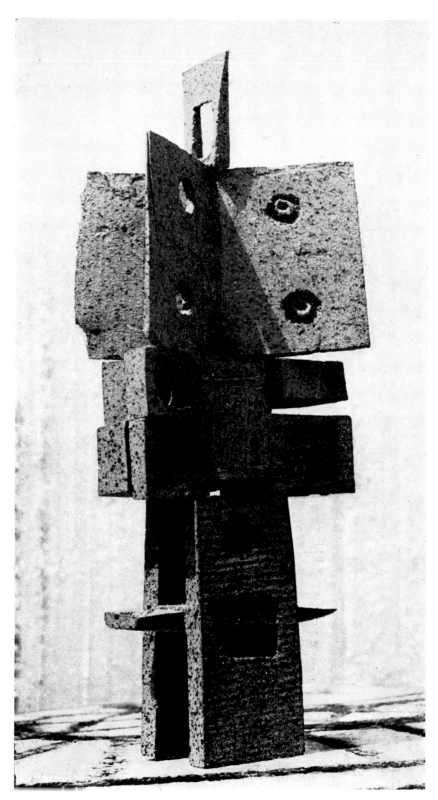

Bryan Newman/46
Oxidised stoneware form with manganese oxide in the clay body. Unglazed. 10″ high.

Eileen Nisbet/47
Earthenware dish with rich amber glaze over incised and painted decoration.
18″×3½″ deep.

Eileen Nisbet/48
Earthenware dish with linear cross and circle design. Rich amber glaze.
17½″×3″ deep.

Eileen Nisbet/49
Earthenware dish with incised linear design. Rich semi-matt yellow glaze. 18″×3½″ deep.

Eileen Nisbet/50
Earthenware dish with black block design, on white matt glaze. 15″ × 2″ deep.

Eileen Nisbet/51
Earthenware dish with leaf design under rich amber glaze. 17½″ × 3″ deep.

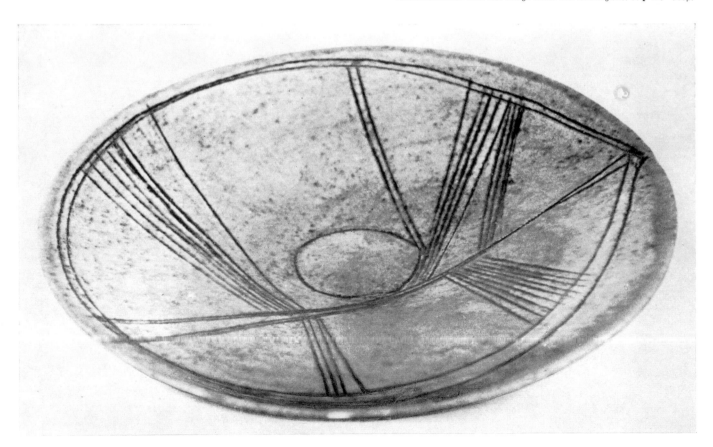

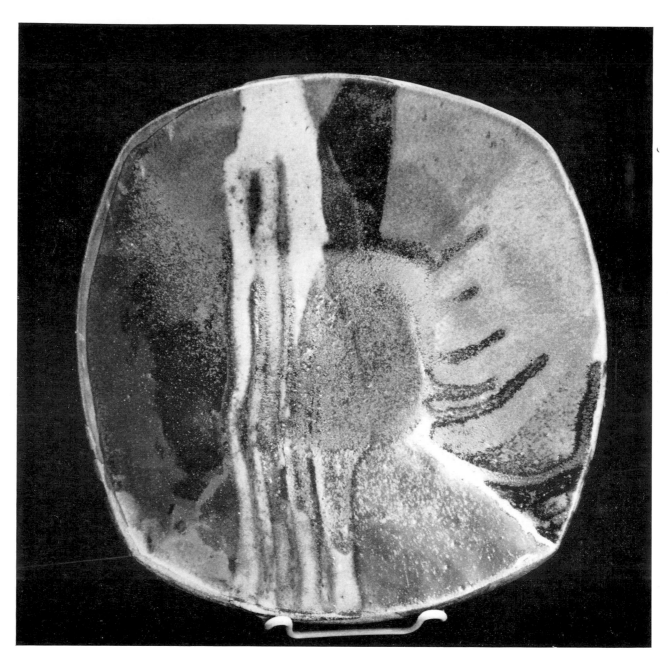

Colin Pearson/52
Stoneware pressed dish with poured glazes over slip decoration. 10″ wide.

Helen Pincombe/53
Large coiled pot with warm-body clay body and rich buff ash-glazed neck

Helen Pincombe/54
Stoneware slab-built pot with
speckled semi-matt glaze. 12″ high.

John Reeve/55
Pressed stoneware dish with Kaki ash glaze. Cone 11 reduction. 14″ wide.

John Reeve/56
Stoneware bottle, press moulded, hand built and thrown with Kaki and tenmoku glazes. Cone 11 reduction. 10″ high.

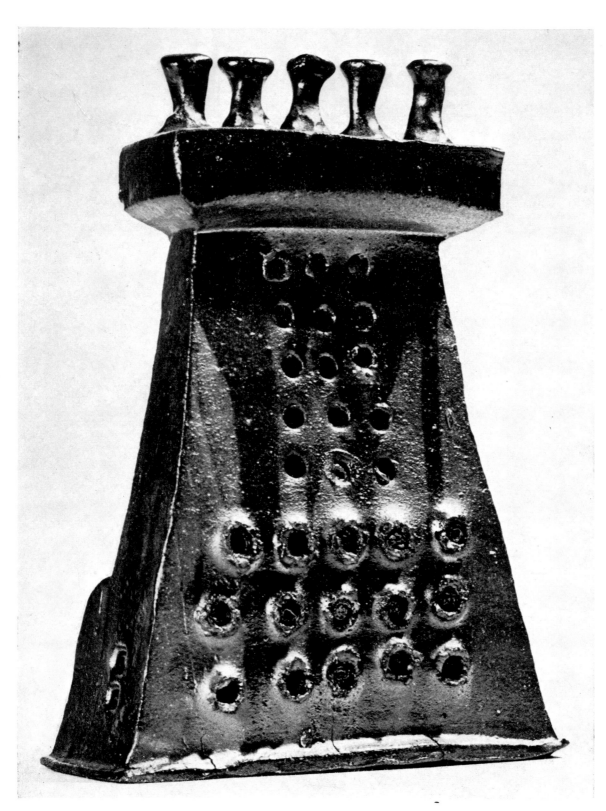

John Reeve/57
Non-mechanical stoneware toy, ash glazed and unglazed surfaces. 10″ high.

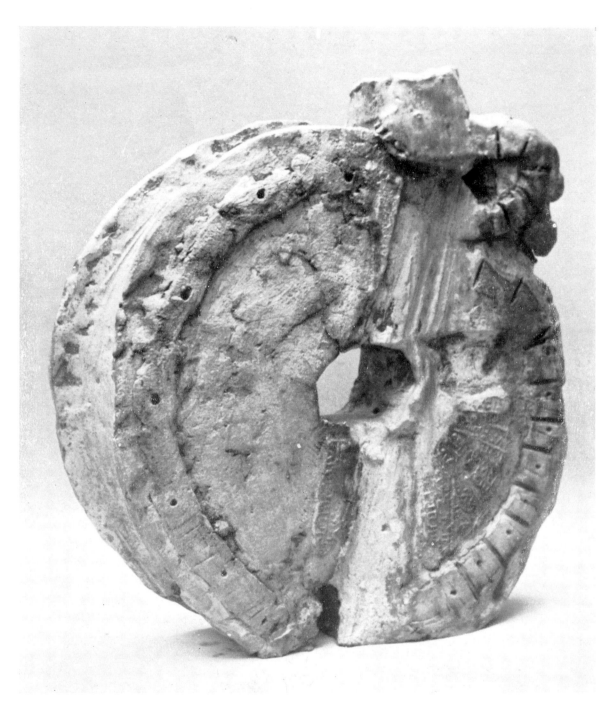

Bernard Rooke/58
Oxidised stoneware wheel form with rubbed-in oxides. 18″ high.

Bernard Rooke/59
Hand built oxidised stoneware pot
with incised design. 9″ high.

Bernard Rooke/60
Hand built oxidised stoneware pot with added clay strips.
Tonal range of warm-clay colours. 24″ high.

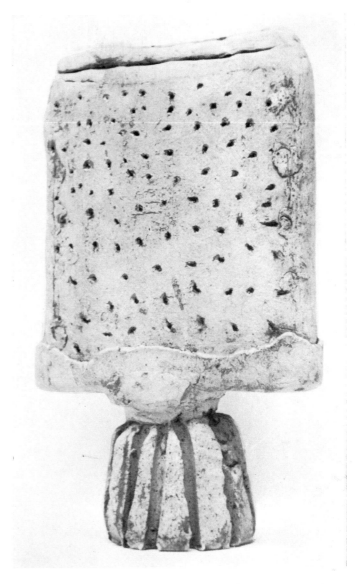

Bernard Rooke/61
Hand built oxidised stoneware form with added and wrapper clays of differing iron colours. 20″ high.

Bernard Rooke/62
Showing reverse side of pot in figure 61.

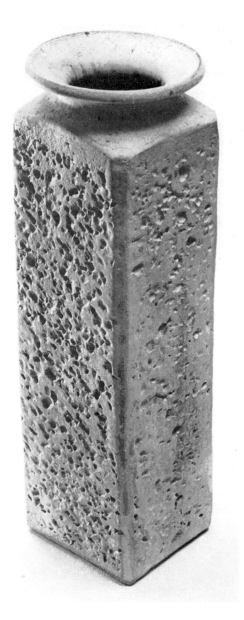

Alan Wallwork/64
Two slab-built stoneware pots with
textured surfaces. Smaller 9″ high.

Anne Thalmessinger/63
Oxidised slab-built stoneware pot with
heavily textured sides. 18″ high.

Alan Wallwork/65
Tall stoneware pot with heavily textured and
oxidised surface under a running off-white glaze.

Alan Wallwork/66
Tall slab-built stoneware pot
with rubbed-in oxides

Alan Wallwork/67
Tall oxidised stoneware pot with areas of textured clay with
rubbed-in copper oxide onto soft-white glaze. Height approx. 24".

Alan Wallwork/68
Two oxidised stoneware pebble pots, grey-white glaze with areas textured and rubbed with oxides.

Alan Wallwork/69
Group of hand built stoneware pots, soft glazes with the textured areas coloured by rubbed-in oxides. Tallest pot 36".

Alan Wallwork/70
Group of hand built stoneware pots. soft glazes with the textured areas coloured by rubbed-in oxides. Tallest pot about 36″ high.

SECTION TWO

WHEELMADE POTTERY, INDIVIDUAL PIECES

SECTION TWO

WHEELMADE POTTERY, INDIVIDUAL PIECES

THE SPINNING action of the wheel dictates a certain range of forms that are both subtle and immensely variable in the hands of the experienced thrower. The thinning skin of clay thrown up by the centrifugal force of the wheel, and contained in shape by the hands of the potter, encloses space, and cuts into space, in a way that no other method does. The tensions of a thrown pot are different from those in one made by handbuilding. The change of method means a change in the sequence of movements used to create the pot. But the vital time element here implied means also a very different state of mind at the moment of creation. A potter working on a wheel brings all his skill, all his sensitivity to form—that is to volume proportion and balance—as well as his feelings for roughness and smoothness, and quick or slow spiralling movements, all these to bear on the clay in order to make the pot in a matter of minutes or even seconds. This immediacy of action leaves a track of the movements made which give a unique life to the thrown pot.

This is why, in a sense, all pots made on the wheel are individual. This section, however, deals with those pots which the potter calls his one-off production. They are not conceived as repetition work although they may derive from it. Experience has shown that it is only when the thrower has fluency that genuine expression in wheel-made pottery becomes possible. In most cases this skill can only be built up by the constant practice that repetition throwing gives. The point here with these individually made thrown pots is that they have been selected because of some special merit. They represent a high point in the potter's achievement, at best having a presence that singles them out from other work. It is surelynow a commonplace but nonetheless true, to say that Bernard Leach's pottery bespeaks a lifetime's devotion to his art—the work has this presence for all who can, to see. No words can define just the quality which makes this salt glazed jug shown on figure 000 such a memorable pot. Then again the flow of pots from such masters as David Leach and Ray Finch have the authority that comes only from complete understanding of the medium. To lift and feel the right balance of a large gently rising and swelling pot by David Leach, and assess the quality of rich iron glaze as it flows over the form, is to enjoy consummate craftsmanship. The strength so apparent in the work of Colin Pearson, to quote one more example, stems from an alliance of skill—the discipline of making and refining over and over again—with an imagination sensitive to form, colour and texture. The work of many potters comes easily to mind; see the salt glazed bottles of Rosemary Wren or a bowl by Gwyn Hanssen. This is the field where individual talent shows most clearly if the skill is there as a vehicle for expression.

Dan Arbeid/71
Stoneware dishes, matt grey-white ash glaze.
Fireclay body warm orange. Incised lines,
inlaid in black pigment. 12″ and 14″ diameter.

Dan Arbeid/72
Four stoneware cylindrical pots
coarse ash glaze,
ochre breaking to rust,
Tallest pot 20″..

Paul Barron/73
Stoneware jug, raw glazed with brown slip glaze and finger combing, thin titanium slip gazel over. 1300° C reduction firing. 10" high.

Paul Barron/74
Stoneware bottle, thrown and beaten. Slate-black glaze with splashes in yellow-brown and green-blue glazes. 7" high.

Paul Barron/76
Stoneware pot, pattern trailed in black slip-glaze on biscuit with very thin buff glaze over, 1300°C reduction firing. 9″ high.

Paul Barron/75
Stoneware pot with four handles at the shoulder, cut and scored pattern, tenmoku glaze. 10″ high.

Paul Barron/77
Tall stoneware bottle, greenish-grey clear gaze,
top dipped twice giving greenish-buff chun. 14″ high.

Michael Buckland/78
Thrown and cut stoneware pot, dark-red body, broken surface
texture, white to rust with celadon mottling. Approx. 7″ high.

Graham Burr/79
Group of three oxidised stoneware pots. Oatmeal coloured ash glazes. 6″, 8″ and 10″ high.

Alan Caiger-Smith/80
Bowl, inside view with brushwork in iron and copper. Wood-fired maiolica. 16½″ diameter.

Alan Caiger-Smith/81
Flower Goblet, maiolica with
brush painting in cobalt and iron.
6¼" high.

Alan Caiger-Smith/82
Bowl, maiolica, with iron and copper brush painting. Wood fired. 16" diameter.

Michael Cardew/83
Three-handled stoneware pot, rich iron brown and grey. 13" high.

Michael Cardew/84
Large stoneware bowl, grey-brown glaze.
11¾" diameter by 6¼" deep.

Michael Cardew/85
Large stoneware tow-handled
teapot, green chun effects in iron glaze.
8½" high, 12½" max. diameter.

Michael Cardew/86
Stoneware plate, black to brown tenmoku glaze with lighter greenish-grey finger wipe decoration. 11″ diameter.

Michael Cardew/88
Stoneware screw-stoppered wine jar, dark iron glaze with touches of
white chun over incised decoration. 14¼″ high.

Michael Cardew/87
Large stoneware dish, brush-painted heron
in iron pigment on light-grey background.

Michael Cardew/89
Two-handled stoneware jar. Medium-grey and iron-brown. 8¾″ high.

Barbara Cass/90
Stoneware cider jar and beakers. Speckled-oatmeal glaze with streaky rust-red brushed areas. 19″ high.

Barbara Cass/91
Stoneware bowl matt-black, light-green
ash glaze. 10" high.

Barbara Cass/92
Stoneware bread bin. Wood-ash glaze
over fireclay. 16" high.

Michael Casson/93
Tall stoneware pot magnesium-grey glaze with rust-red brush painting. 32" high.

Michael Casson/94
Stoneware wine jar, tenmoku glaze
cut sides. 13½" high.

Michael Casson/95
Oxidised stoneware pot with added lugs. Rough red body
and smooth grey white glaze. 20" high.

Michael Casson/97
Oxidised stoneware jug.
Rough red body, smooth grey white glaze with
yellow to black iron brush painting.
8″ high.

Michael Casson/96
Stoneware pot with 'landscape'
decoration in added clay.
Grey to white reduced dolomite glaze.
18″ high, 20″ diameter.

M

Ken Clark and Ann Wynn Reeves/98
Earthenware pot—textured and patterned surface with
applied oxides—tin glaze and coloured glazes.
12″ high, 9″ diameter.

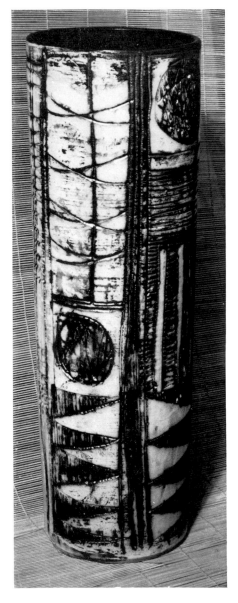

Ken Clark and Anne Wynn Reeves/99
Tall earthenware pot with incised decoration and
applied oxides under a tin glaze and coloured glazes.
24″ high

Ken Clark and Ann Wynn Reeves/100
Group of three earthenware pots, red body with incised decoration under tin glaze. Tallest 24″ high.

Derek Clarkson/101
Stoneware cylinders with applied clay decoration. Titanium and iron felspathic glaze. 1300°C. 12″ and 13″ high.

Derek Clarkson/102
Stoneware bowl, wood-ash glaze cream colour.
Wax-resist decoration with rust iron slip glaze. 1300°C.
12″ diameter.

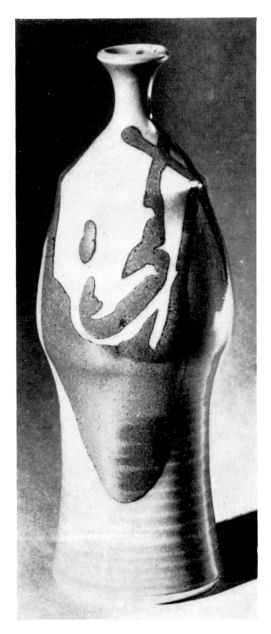

Derek Clarkson/103
Stoneware bottle, white body celadon glaze decoration
by wax resists and poured Kaku glaze. 1300°C.

Walter Cole/104
Stoneware dishes, light buff body
painted in iron on light grey ground.
5″ diameter.

Walter Cole/105
Stoneware plate with creamy grey
glaze fish painted in soft iron brown.
6″ diameter.

Joanna Constantinidis/107
Porcelain teapot, soft white glaze and iron bands. 6″ high.

Joanna Constantinidis/106
Fluted stoneware pot grey-green
ash glaze. 4½″ high.

Joanna Constantinidis/108
Large stoneware bowl, incised decoration and burnt iron rim. White speckled glaze inside. 14″ diameter.

Hans Coper/100
Stoneware pot, metallic black glaze. 6″ high.

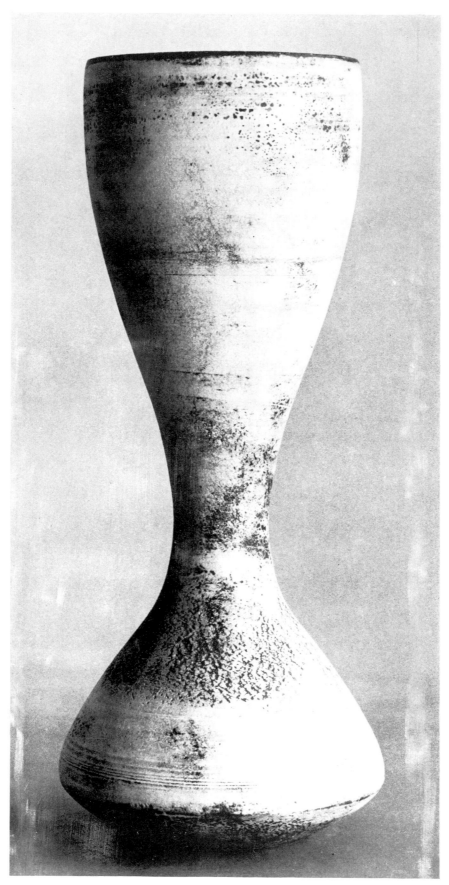

Hans Coper/110
Stoneware pot, white glaze over engobes. 17″ high.

Hans Coper/111
Stoneware pot, matt white glaze over engobes. 5″ high.

Hans Coper/112
Stoneware pot, matt white glaze over engobes. 14″ high.

Hans Coper/113
Stoneware bottle, white glaze over engobes. 5″ high.

Hans Coper/114
Stoneware pot, matt white glaze over engobes. 5″ high.

Derek Emms/117
Stoneware vase cut sided panels, tenmoku glaze black breaking to rust. 1300°C.

Derek Emms/118
Fluted stoneware teapot, tenmoku glaze. 1300°C.

Murray Fieldhouse/119
Oxidised stoneware serving platter.
Wood ash and black poured glazes.
1240° C. 12″ diameter.

Murray Fieldhouse/120
Nut bowl and Dutch gin bottle.
Oxidised wood ash and iron glaze
simulating tea dust. 1240°C.
Bowl 6″ diameter.

Tessa Fuchs/121
Two earthenware bottles. Tall bottle mid-green matt glaze, 7½″ high. Bottle with cut edges apple-green matt glaze, 3½″ high.

Alan Spencer Green/122
Small stoneware bowl with matt white glaze and reduced copper red decoration. 5″ diameter.

Alan Spencer Green/123
Small lidded stoneware pot, saturated with iron manganese and cobalt to fire slate grey. 6″ diameter.

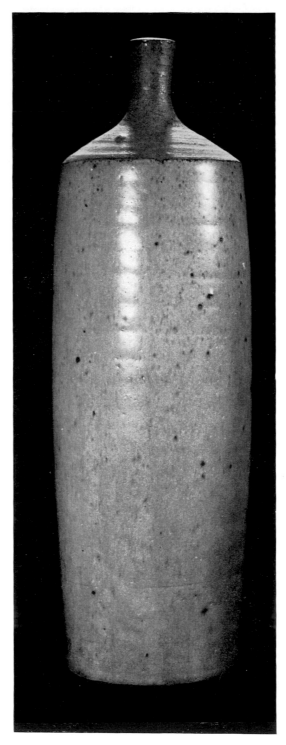

Arthur Griffiths/124
Tall stoneware bottle with unglazed neck and smooth warm buff-
grey body glaze. 18″ high.

Henry Hammond/125
Tall vase with brush painted decoration. 14½″ × 7½″.

Henry Hammond/126
Porcelain bowl with fish design in cobalt blue. 9″ × 7½″

Henry Hammond/127
Small stoneware bowl with painted reed decoration on a white background, reduction firing. $3\frac{1}{2}'' \times 2\frac{1}{2}''$.

Henry Hammond/128
Round stoneware pot with bamboo design in iron on celadon green glaze. 3″ high.

Gwyn Hanssen/129
Group of three small creamy white
porcelain bowls and a footed dark brown
stoneware bowl with iron markings·
Oxidised 1250°C. Sizes 3″–4″ diameter·

Anita Hoy/130
Earthenware teapot, black and white slip over red body
semi-transparent glaze, 1060°C. 6″ diameter.

Anita Hoy/131
Earthenware teapot, black and white slip
over red body, semi-transparent glaze,
1060°C. 6″ diameter.

Bernard Leach/132
Fluted stoneware bottle, black to rust tenmoku glaze. 10″ high.

Bernard Leach/133
Salte glaze jug. 8″ high.

Bernard Leach/134
Tall stoneware bottle, brush work in iron over white hakeme.

Bernard Leach/135
Small white porcelain covered pot, with cut feet

Bernard Leach/136
Stoneware pot with sgraffito decoration under a semi-transparent glaze. 7″ high.

Bernard Leach/137
Small stoneware pot with slip decoration, made at Mashiko

Janet Leach/138
Large stoneware vase with reduced white glaze decoration. 14″×16″.

Janet Leach/139
Squared stoneware bowl with unglazed exterior. $6\frac{1}{2}'' \times 14''$.

Janet Leach/140
Grey and white oval stoneware bottle. 9½″ high.

David Leach/141
Fluted grey glazed earthenware bowl. 8″ diameter.

David Leach/142
Stoneware bowl with unusual glaze effects of variegated mottling. 8″ diameter.

Trentham de Leliva/143
Corked oxidised stoneware jar with dolomite glaze over iron and cobalt slip. 13' high,

Eileen Lewenstein/144
Tall oxidised stoneware vase brushed with coarse slip and 'turnings' thrown on.

Victor Margrie/145

Three small bowls in white stoneware body. Sprigged and cut decoration. White barium glaze inside, exterior left unglazed. 4″ diameter.

Victor Margrie/146
Oxidised one-pint stoneware teapot. Oatmeal glaze with inlaid black slip and incised decoration.

Victor Margrie/147
One-pint teapot, dark blue barium glaze.

Reginald Marlow/148
Stoneware bowl, tenmoku glaze under chun glaze giving a broken texture. 8¾″ diameter.

Reginald Marlow/149
Stoneware cylindrical vase. Wood ash glaze with wax resist decoration and iron pigment. 12½″ high.

Ray Marshall/150
Tall oxidised stoneware bottle, with added pierced lugs, 18″ high approx.; and stoneware bottle with fluted 3-tier girdle, approx. 12″ high.

Ray Marshall/151
Three oxidised stoneware bottles with incised lines and circles. Approx. 12″ high.

William Marshall/152
White porcelain vase, with cut sides.
7″ high.

Paul Metcalfe/153
Tall reduced stoneware bird pot, grey breaking to
brown rust with darker iron painting.
Approx. 18″ high.

Denis Moore/154
Two stoneware pots reduced, grey breaking to rust red and celadon, wood ash glazed. Taller pot 9″ high.

Colin Pearson/155
Large stoneware plate, thin iron slip with felspathic glaze and poured white glaze. 20″ diameter.

Colin Pearson/156
Stoneware jar glazed at the top in a rich tenmoku under a fatty grey-white glaze. 9″ high.

Helen Pincombe/157
Group of three stoneware bowls: (*a*) iron painting; (*b*) beaten and cut sides; (*c*) dark greeny-brown glaze. Largest 8″ high.

Helen Pincombe/158
Stoneware bowl with speckled iron bearing body breaking through the off-white glaze. Iron painting. 8″ high.

Stoneware dish, fluted, light buff wood ash glaze. 12″ diameter.

Gordon Plahn/160
Group of four small stoneware pots with varied iron glazes. Approx. 6″ high.

Katherine Pleydell-Bouverie/161
Oxidised stoneware bowl, incised clay under a cream-grey glaze. 4″ high.

Katherine Pleydell-Bouverie/162
Oxidised stoneware bottle with fluted sides. Tenmoku glaze. 4″ high.

Thomas Plowman/163
Oxidised stoneware bowl, oatmeal glaze, wax resist dark blue slip decoration. 8″ wide.

Thomas Plowman/164
Oxidised lidded jar, speckled blue with poured tenmoku glaze, wax resist decoration. 10″ high.

John Reeve/165
Vase, clay-ash glaze, thrown, reduced stoneware, cone 10. 17″ high.

John Reeve/166
Stoneware vase with clay and ash glaze, cone 11. 12″ high

Lucie Rie/167
Stoneware bottle with off-white matt glaze on blue-black body. 8″ high.

Lucie Rie/168
Porcelain bottle, sgraffito inside and outside. Blue lines on unglazed bands on the outside. 9″ high.

Lucie Rie/169
Porcelain pot wity lines cut in,
matt-white glaze. 4″ high.

Lucie Rie/170
Porcelain bowl, sgraffito inside, outside unglazed with black lines inlaid. 4″ high.

Lucie Rie/171
Porcelain bowl, lines cut in matt white glaze. 3¼″ high.

Lucie Rie/172
Stoneware bottle, off-white matt glaze
on dark-brown body. 9½" high.

Anne Thalmessinger/173
Stoneware plant pot with cut slip decoration. 8″×6″ approx.

Geoffrey Whiting/174
Reduced stoneware bottle. Pattern combed in soft clay, raw glazed with olive green running ash glaze over iron wash. 9″ high.

Denis Wren/175
Thrown and beaten salt glazed pot with added clay lug, variegated blue glazed
effects. 12″ high.

Denise Wren/176
Salt-glazed jars and bottle. Variegated glaze effects. Tallest approx. 8″.

Denise Wren/177
Group of salt glazed pots, decorated in the damp clay through oxides. 1310°C.

Rosemary Wren/178
Two stoneware bottles; *Left,* with poured pattern of brilliant turqouise glaze. *Right,* dry brown wood ash and kaolin pourings; both gas kiln reduction, 1300°C.

Rosemary Wren/179
Thrown and flattened salt glaze stoneware bottle with wood ash and kaolin green-grey pourings on speckled golden brown. Coke kiln reduction 1300°C. 14″ high.

SECTION THREE

WHEELMADE POTTERY, REPETITION PRODUCTION

SECTION THREE

WHEELMADE POTTERY, REPETITION PRODUCTION

THERE ARE relatively few potters in this group at the present time, but it is true to say that they include some of the most experienced in the country. The best domestic pottery of this type is functionally sound and aesthetically rewarding; it radiates its own particular kind of life. To have, and use in the home, articles made by the individual craftsmen is manifestly a constant joy to a growing number of people. Consequently the demand for good domestic table-ware made by hand methods has increased to such an extent that it outstrips the supply. But just because of the special skills and disciplines needed in this kind of production the situation will not be easily resolved. To make tea and coffee sets, oven ware of all kinds, and all the many other usable items, by hand, and earn a suitable living from such enterprise demands a workshop knowledge as well as a temperament of a special type.

Prices can only be kept at a reasonable level—thus ensuring that those who want to buy can do so—by watching every phase of the workshop's management. This concern has led some to use local clays and materials for their relative cheapness, as well as their character. But even more than this the workshop economy has led to a directness of method and simplicity of approach to shape and decoration on the part of these potters who wish their work to be within reach of all. Fortunately there has always been a school of thought that sees this economic necessity as an aesthetic virtue. They would want to make pots in no other way. Two examples to represent potters whose work seems to express this attitude would be Ray Finch and Richard Batterham. Ray Finch's Winchcombe pottery is a larger workshop producing a greater range of forms—plates of all sizes, coffee and tea sets, casseroles, cider jars, the whole gamut of domestic ware in fact—but both share the quality of unpretentious craftsmanship. Richard Batterham's use of simple cutting and incising beneath the felspathic high fired glaze has an appealing directness. It may stem ultimately from the East, just as Ray Finch's use of trailed glaze on his stoneware casserole has its origin in seventeeth century English slipware, but at best both potters' work has that timeless quality to which most potters aspire.

That there are, and always have been, potters holding the opposite views only adds to the general scope and, I believe strength, of pottery made in this country today. This variety is a reflection of the many strands of thought stretching from William Morris and Bernard Leach to the protagonists of Industrial design, that have gone to make up British pottery.

Richard Batterham/180
Stoneware coffee jug with added lip,
dark celadon glaze.
Height 8½".

Richard Batterham/181
Stoneware store jars with
unglazed rims, celadon glaze.
Smaller jar height 4".

Richard Batterham/182
Stoneware store jar, impressed decoration. Tenmoku glaze on pot, celadon glaze on lid and inside.
Height 6½".

Richard Batterham/183
Cut sided stoneware teapot, celadon glaze. Height 5".

Boscean Pottery/184
Stoneware jug and two bowls. Jug 9¾″ high with warm brown glaze. Bowl left, dark brown over grey with wax resist, height 3¾″. Bowl right semi-transparent celadon, height 3¼″.

Boscean Pottery/185
Stoneware bowl with ash glaze over iron. Diameter 6″, height 4″

Alan Caiger-Smith/186
Large and medium maiolica casseroles with copper, cobalt and iron painting. Diameters 8″, 9½″.

Alan Caiger-Smith/187
1½ gallon maiolica
wood-fired teapot,
iron and copper painting.
Height 9″.

Alan Caiger-Smith/188
Set of six maiolica goblets painted in copper and cobalt oxides. Height 6″.

Michael Casson/189
Stoneware store jar,
reduced dolomite glaze
with banded tenmoku and iron.
Height 10″.

Michael Casson/190
Group of domestic stoneware, two-pint green ash glazed coffee pot with mug. Three-pint teapot, speckled cream glaze with vitreous iron slip decoration.

Sheila Casson/191
Part of a stoneware tea set with medium brown ash glaze and rust red iron decoration. Teapot 1½ pints.

Sheila Casson/192
Stoneware two-pint casseroles, reduced dolomite glaze with iron speckle.

Sheila Casson/193
Stoneware 1½ pint teapot, tenmoku glaze with brushed iron decoration.

Sheila Casson/194
Stoneware half-pint mugs reduced dolomite glaze and wax resist decoration.

Ken Clark/195
Earthenware slip-cast beakers with rich amber-yellow glaze and copper painting, white tin glaze inside. Tallest 10″.

David Eeles/196
Earthenware casserole slipware, brown, black, and white slip under a transparent glaze.

David Eeles/197
Six-pint earthenware jug, slip ware.

David Eeles/198
Ten-pint earthenware jug, slip ware.

Ray Finch/199
Group of domestic stoneware. Two-pint coffee and teapots, jug. cups and saucers and sugar bowl. Off-white talc glaze with iron speckle.

Ray Finch/200
Five-pint stoneware casserole, dark rust red iron glaze with trailed white glaze decoration.

Ray Finch/201
Group of standard Winchcombe stoneware with off-white talc glaze. Unglazed exterior to casserole.

Robert Fournier/202
Oxidised stoneware casseroles, black glaze with unglazed knobs and rims.

Robert Fournier/203
Part of oxidised stoneware coffee set, wax resist decoration with grey-blue banding.

Annette Fuchs/204
Earthenware coffee set, dark purple-brown matt glaze over red body. Coffee pot 10″ high.

Annette Fuchs/205
Two earthenware oil bottles, dark purple-brown matt glaze over red body. 5″ high.

Gwyn Hanssen/206
1½ pint stoneware casserole, grey-green glaze with grey-brown markings. 7″ diameter.

Gwyn Hanssen/207
Two one-pint and one quart stoneware jugs, flashed feet where exposed to wood ash in the kiln. *Left,* opaque soft grey ; *centre,* dark olive transparent ; *right,* grey-brown glaze. 11 , 6¼ , 6¼"

Gwyn Hanssen/208
1 ½ pint stoneware teapots,
wood fired transparent glaze;
Right, steely grey opaque glaze
reduction atmosphere.
Left, blue-grey.

Gwyn Hanssen/209
Large stoneware bowl, grey-green transparent glaze, and flashed brick-red feet. Incised decoration on the outside. 18" diameter.

Harry Horlock-Stringer/210
Set of children's earthenware cups with sprigs and slipped rims, red body, tin glaze.

Harry Horlock-Stringer/211
Set of children's earthenware
first plates with sprigs and
slipped rims. Red body, tin glaze.

Harry Horlock-Stringer/212
Oxidised stoneware casserole,
soft off-white glaze over
dark ovenware body. Iron band on lid.

David Leach/213
Set of 3 jugs and 6 mugs. Stoneware ash glaze, brushed iron and cobalt decoration. 1280°C.
Set of three jugs and six mugs. Stoneware ash glaze, brushed iron and cobalt decoration. 1280°C.

David Leach/214
One-gallon store jar, black breaking to rust, tenmoku glaze. 1300 °C.

David Leach/215
Fluted stoneware teapot, 2 pint,
off-white oatmeal colour
slightly speckly matt glaze.
1270° C.

David Leach/214
Three-pint stoneware teapot.
Mattish oatmeal glaze
with brush decoration
in iron and cobalt.
1280°C.

Leach pottery standard ware/217–221
217: bowls and plates, various glazes from celadon to tenmoku. **218:** ovenware, unglazed exteriors. **219:** ovenware individual soup dishes, sauce boat and egg bakers, all with unglazed exteriors. **220:** one-pint mug with other standard mugs and two-pint jug. **221:** stoneware jugs ½ to 2 pint capacity.

Trentham de Leliva/222
Stoneware coffee jug 9″ high and stoneware teapot 5″ high. Both oxidised dark-rust-green ash glaze.

John Maltby/223
Group of **three** stoneware lidded pots. Smaller ones 3½″ diameter. Two with tenmoku glazes, other with heavily speckled oatmeal glaze with iron painting.

Colin Pearson/224
Large stoneware casserole, reduced dolomite glaze with iron speckle.

Colin Pearson/225
Group of stoneware. Two sizes of cup and saucer. Two sizes of covered jug and one other jug. All dipped in slip under a felspathic glaze. Bottom half of all pots unglazed.

Colin Pearson/226
Very large stoneware casserole with fat off-white glaze breaking to red-brown where underneath iron glaze shows through.

John Reeve/227
Stoneware jar with cut sides and squared top
dipped at the top with ash glaze. Cone 10.
5″ high.

John Reeve/228
Stoneware bowl reduced felspar clay
and ash glaze. 14″ wide.

John Reeve/229
Stoneware jug reduced kaki glaze with poured tenmoku glaze on top. Cone 11. 9″ high.

John Reeve/230
Stoneware casserole reduced green glaze. 10″ wide.

Lucie Rie/231
Standard oxidised stoneware teapot with brushed manganese on the outside. 5″ high.

Margaret Shotton/232
Group of oxidised stoneware, matt yellow and rust browns to green ash glazes.

Margaret Shotton/233
Oxidised stoneware casseroles, rust brown to green ash glazes.

John Solly/234
One pint and 2½ pint earthenware casseroles. Low solubility tine glaze inside, matt zircon glaze outside. 1150° C.

John Solly/235
Half-pint earthenware mug. Transparent iron glaze over blue combed slip.

Marianne de Trey/236
Wide stoneware dish with opaque glaze scraped away to leave brown unglazed surfaces on uncut edges. 11″ diameter.

Marianne de Trey/237
Two stoneware flower pot holders,
7″ diameter. One very dark oxidised glaze
the other fluting under a white glaze.

Marianne de Trey/238
Stoneware bowls, with fluted decoration
under a white oxidised glaze.
Diameters 3″, 4″ and 6″.

Marianne de Trey/239
Two stoneware vases thrown, with cut sides. *Left,* wood ash glaze. *Right,* tenmoku with white glaze streak, 9" high.

Marianne de Trey/240
Porcelain bowl with incised decoration. 4″ diameter.

Marianne de Trey/241
Porcelain bowl white and tenmoku glazes. 5″ diameter.

Geoffrey Whiting/242
Group of stoneware tableware with two-pint teapot. Licht speckled reduced glaze.

Geoffrey Whiting/243
Stoneware pouring bowl, unglazed exterior, burnt brown smooth celadon glaze inside. 6″ diameter.

INDEX TO POTTERS